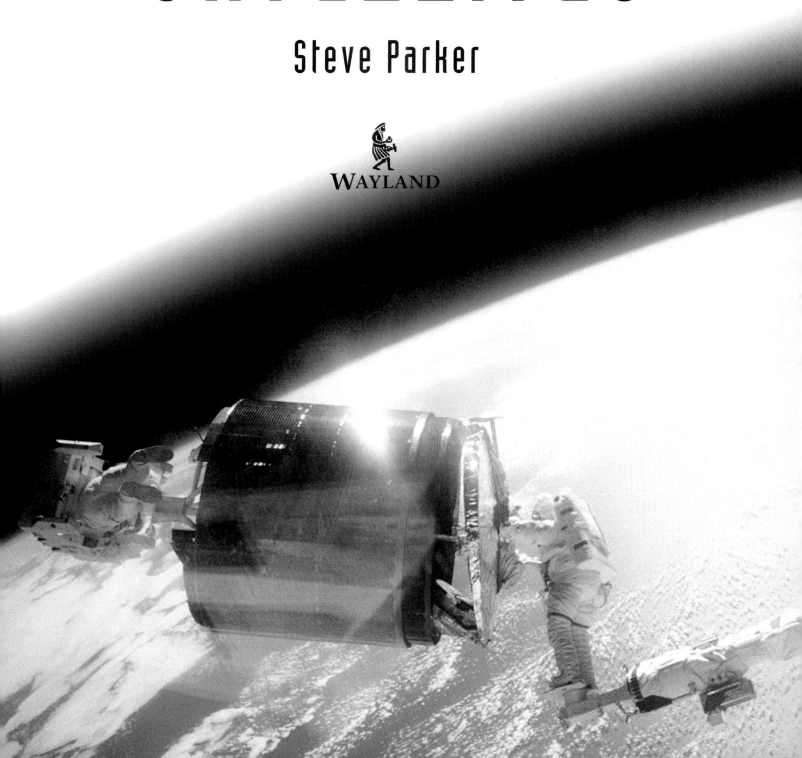

20th Century Inventions

SATELLITES

Steve Parker

WAYLAND

20th Century Inventions

COMPUTERS

LASERS

SATELLITES

TELECOMMUNICATIONS

Cover and title page: A communications satellite is launched from the Space Shuttle *Discovery*.

Series and book editor: Paul Bennett
Series designer: Tim Mayer
Book designer: Paul Bennett

First published in 1996 by Wayland Publishers Limited,
61 Western Road, Hove, East Sussex BN3 1JD, England

British Library Cataloguing in Publication Data
Parker, Steve, 1952
    Satellites. – (Twentieth century inventions)
    1. Artificial satellites – Juvenile literature
    I. Title
    629.4'6

ISBN 0 7502 1792 8

Typeset by Paul Bennett
Printed and bound in Italy by G. Canale & C.S.p.A., Turin

Picture acknowledgements
Aspect Picture Library 12/NASA; Ann Ronan Picture Library 24; Image Select 33, 39/NASA; Ole Steen Hansen, Forlaget Flachs 27; Rex Features 8; Science Photo Library cover and title page/NASA, 4/NASA, 5/NOAA, 6/NASA, 7 (top)/Jack Finch, 10/European Space Agency, 14/NASA, 16, 18/Jerome Yeats, 19 (top)/Tony Buxton, 19 (bottom)/Mikki Rain, 22/James Stevenson, 26/David Parker, 28/David Parker, 29/Julian Baum, 30/CNES, 1988 Distribution SPOT Image, 32/Ducros/ Jerrican, 34 (both)/NASA, 35/Dr Seth Shostak, 36/NASA, 37/Max Planck Institut Fur Extraterrestrische Physik, 38/Novosti, 41/Erik Viktor, 42/Jerry Manson, 43/Space Telescope Science Institute/NASA, 44 (top)/NASA, 45 (top left); Telegraph Colour Library 9 (top), 9 (bottom)/Dilip Mehta, 44 (middle); The Image Bank 20, 25 (bottom), 45 (top right), 45 (bottom); Topham 7 (bottom), 23/Associated Press, 40/Associated Press, 44 (bottom). Artwork on pages 11, 13, 15, 17, 21, 25, 31 (top) by Tim Benké, Top Draw (Tableaux). All other pictures Wayland Picture Library.

20th Century Inventions
CONTENTS

INTRODUCTION

An *Intelsat VI* communications satellite rushes on its lonely, silent, never-ending orbit, above Earth's clouds. After adjustment by the Space Shuttle *Endeavour*, it will boost into a far higher orbit.

Have you ever seen a satellite? Perhaps you've seen one in a museum or exhibition. Or you may have glimpsed one in the sky at night, without realizing – a tiny speck of light that looks like a slowly moving star.

Most satellites are out of sight, far above us in the darkness and silence of space. Yet they are a vital part of our modern world, and they are becoming more numerous and more important every year. In this book you can read about how satellites are involved in hundreds of day-to-day events in our homes, schools, offices and factories, whether we are at work or play, or on the move.

Satellites in daily life

When you watch television, you may be seeing pictures that have been sent from another country and are then beamed by satellites around the world. If you watch satellite television, the programmes come from a satellite directly to your home. When you make a long-distance telephone call, or link your computer to another one by the telephone line, you may well be using at least one satellite.

Satellites in industry and research

The very latest news about trade, shares and prices can be sent via satellite almost instantly between the world's finance centres. Satellite photographs of the Earth help to plan for land use, such as where to grow crops, plant forests, dam rivers and build roads, railways and towns.

Scientists and researchers also use satellites to peer outwards, into deep space. They study planets, stars and galaxies to reveal the secrets of the universe. And every day, military 'spy satellites' watch over the world. You may not have seen a satellite, but a satellite has probably seen you.

What is a satellite?

A satellite is something that goes around, or orbits, something else. For example, the Earth is a satellite of the Sun, and the Moon is a satellite of the Earth. These are natural satellites. When a spacecraft such as the Space Shuttle is launched, it becomes a satellite of the Earth, too.

In everyday speech, 'satellite' usually means an unmanned artificial object that orbits the Earth. If the object has people or other living things on board, it is usually called a spacecraft or space vehicle.

The *NOAA-6* weather satellite spies hurricane Diana approaching the USA's east coast, in 1984.

THE FIRST SATELLITES

The idea of a satellite was first suggested more than 300 years ago, by the scientist Isaac Newton. He realized that the Earth's gravity held the Moon in its orbit, as a natural satellite of the Earth. In 1687, Newton suggested that an artificial satellite could do the same. Scientists today still use Newton's laws of motion to make sure a satellite stays up (see page 15).

Rocket scientist Robert Goddard teaching students at Clark University in 1924, two years before he launched the first rocket. It travelled only 56 metres – but it was a start.

Rockets

Before you can have a satellite in space, you need a rocket to put it there. In 1926 the first modern-style, liquid-fuel rocket was launched by the US scientist Robert Goddard. By 1954, scientists knew how to build rockets powerful enough to reach space.

The space race

In the 1950s, the two superpowers of the time, USA and USSR, raced to get ahead in science and technology. The USSR won the first victory. On 4 October 1957, they launched the first object into space – the satellite, *Sputnik 1*. People all around the world were amazed. The Space Age had begun.

Sputnik 1

The first satellite was a shiny metal ball about a metre across, weighing 83 kilogrammes. It had four long antennae (aerials) for sending radio signals from its radio beacon. *Sputnik 1* orbited the Earth at heights of 100–300 kilometres and stayed in space for six months. Then it gradually fell back to Earth and burned up in the high atmosphere as the first artificial 'shooting star'.

The shimmering, glowing curtains of the Northern and Southern Lights (auroras) have been studied by satellites passing through them, more than 100 kilometres above Earth's surface.

Below **Laika, the world's first space traveller, lived inside the sealed air-filled capsule of the satellite *Sputnik 2*.**

First creature in space

There were several more *Sputnik* satellites. *Sputnik 2* was launched in November 1957, carrying the first living thing into space – a dog, Laika. She survived inside the capsule, showing that life could exist in the conditions of space. But *Sputnik 2* was not designed to come back to Earth. After ten days, Laika was quietly put to sleep.

Explorer

The USA soon followed the USSR into space. Its first satellite, *Explorer 1*, was launched in January 1958 from Cape Canaveral, Florida, and was one of the first in a series of satellites built to do similar jobs. This is called a satellite programme. *Explorer 6* sent back the first television pictures of clouds far below, shrouding the Earth. *Explorer 35* discovered that the Moon, unlike the Earth, has no magnetism of its own. The Explorer programme is still making new scientific discoveries today.

The first communication satellites

People around the world followed the exciting start of the Space Age with the launch of the Russian satellite, *Sputnik 1* in October 1957. But gradually, satellites faded from the news. More and more were being launched by both the USA and Russia, but they were mainly for space research, and they did not affect people's daily lives.

The Beatles pop group sing *All You Need Is Love* in England, on the first worldwide live television satellite link-up. The show on 25 June 1967 was watched by an estimated 400 million people.

Telstar 1

Then, in 1962, there was a new satellite sensation. *Telstar 1* was launched on 10 July, by a Delta rocket from the US space base of Cape Canaveral. The same day, it relayed (sent on) radio signals from the USA to Europe. These radio signals were for television pictures, and made history as the first live broadcast across the Atlantic Ocean.

Today, we are used to television pictures beamed instantly by satellites from anywhere in the world. In 1962, people in Europe gathered around their television sets and watched open-mouthed as pictures came 'live' across the Atlantic.

These televison pictures were sent to *Telstar 1* by a ground station in the north-west USA. The satellite received them, boosted the signals, and sent them back down to ground stations in Europe. The pictures were then broadcast by the usual ground-based transmitters to people's homes.

Telstar 2, launched in 1963, was 87 centimetres across. The dark panels are solar cells, turning sunlight into electricity to charge its batteries. It handled one television channel or six telephone lines.

Telstar 1 had a low elliptical orbit (see page 13). It was only in the correct position to relay its signals for a short period of time on each orbit, so the television programmes had to be specially made to fit into these time slots. Also, its equipment could cope with only one black-and-white television channel. Despite these limitations, *Telstar 1* was an instant hit. There was even a chart-topping pop song named after it by a group called the Tornadoes.

One person's vision

In an article in *Wireless World* in 1945, scientist and writer Arthur C Clark suggested that satellites could carry out global communications. He proposed the geostationary orbit for 'satellite repeaters' that would receive and send on radio signals. It was as though the satellite was a normal radio receiver-transmitter, but on an incredibly tall radio mast 36,000 kilometres high. He called the article 'Extra-Terrestrial Relays'. Some people laughed at the time – but it has largely come true.

HOW SATELLITES WORK

Making a satellite

Most modern satellites have the same basic parts, plus extra equipment depending on what job they do. The basic parts include a radar system to measure the height from the Earth's surface, and receivers and transmitters to pick up and send out signals – usually radio waves or microwaves. There are small attitude control nozzles, also called thrusters or 'puffers'. These squirt out puffs of gas to tilt the satellite and change its attitude or position, so that it always faces the correct way.

Power

The satellite needs a power source for its electrical equipment. This usually comes from large fold-out panels containing thousands of solar cells, which turn the energy of sunlight into electricity. However, for half of its orbit, the satellite is in shadow, on the side of the Earth away from the Sun, so solar power alone is not sufficient. For this reason, most satellites carry small, lightweight batteries. These are recharged by the solar panels, and continue the work of powering the satellite's equipment during the hours in darkness.

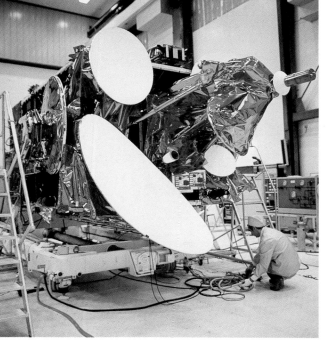

Technicians check and adjust an Olympus satellite, one of many in the European Space Agency's (ESA) programme. The special assembly room is as clean as a hospital operating theatre.

Other equipment

Each satellite has other equipment. A research satellite may have telescopes and antennae pointing outwards, to receive rays from deep in space. A survsat (survey satellite) has telescopes, cameras and other sensors pointing down, to view the Earth's surface. A comsat (communication satellite) has various antennae and thousands of transponders (automatic devices used to receive and send on radio signals), each one dealing with a radio or telephone channel, or perhaps part of a television channel.

These pieces of equipment are designed and built by electronics experts and aerospace engineers. They have built up a great amount of experience and knowledge, and satellite operators can choose from various designs and layouts. Some satellite makers sell their products to users as a commercial business. You can buy one 'off the peg', which takes about one or two years to build, and costs about US$15 (£10) million. Or you can have a satellite specially designed for your needs, which might take twice as long and cost five times more. The satellite business is very, very costly.

Intelsat IV **comsats, launched from the 1970s, were more than 5 metres tall. At the top are the communications and control antennae. In the upper body are spoke-like boxes of electronics, and four pear-shaped attitude 'puffers'. The main rocket nozzle is at the base, and solar panels cover the cylindrical body.**

1 Command antenna
2 Wide-beam antennae
3 Spot-beam dish antenna
4 Electronics circuit cases
5 Puffer jets
6 Solar panels
7 Battery pack ring
8 Main rocket engine nozzle

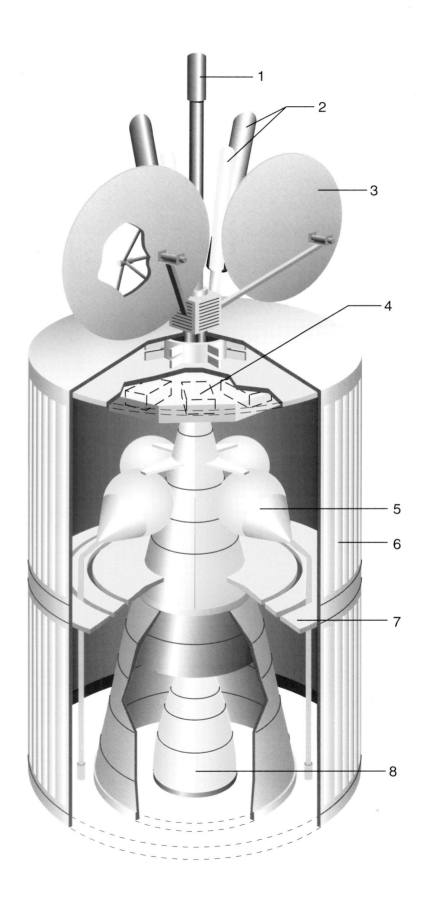

Launching a satellite

An Atlas Centaur rocket blasts off at Cape Canaveral, carrying an *Intelsat V* comsat that will eventually 'hover' 36,000 kilometres above the Atlantic Ocean.

The first comsat, *Telstar 1*, was about the size and weight of an adult person curled up tight. A modern comsat like *Intelsat VI* is bigger than a luxury limousine and weighs 2 tonnes. It takes a powerful rocket to lift it into space. The rocket is called the ELV (expendable launch vehicle) and the satellites and other items it carries are the payload. After the launch, the rocket drifts away into space or falls to Earth and burns up.

The US Space Shuttle is an RLV (reuseable launch vehicle). Once it has launched its payload in space, it can return to Earth to be used again. Not only can the Space Shuttle take up two or more satellites at the same time, it can also 'catch' already orbiting satellites for repair or bring them back to Earth.

The satellite's antennae, solar panels and other parts that stick out are usually folded up for launch, so that they take up less room. When the satellite is released, they unfold into their working positions.

Deployment

The satellite is released and its systems checked. It may have a small rocket or payload assist motor that boosts it into its final orbital position, depending on its task.

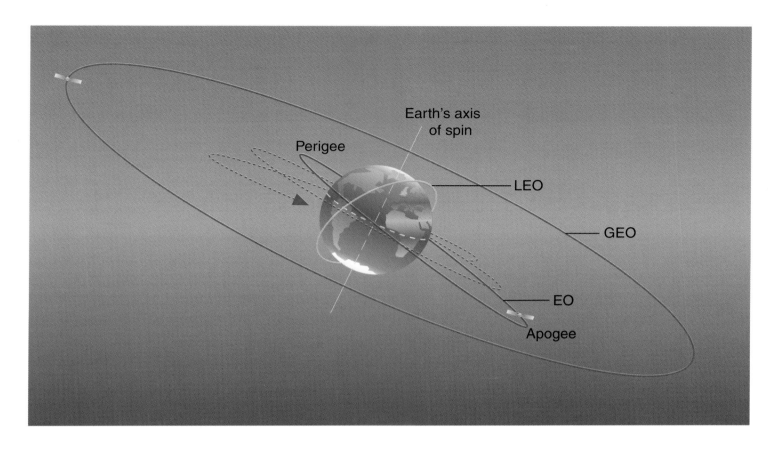

Low Earth orbit (LEO) is relatively close to our planet. Geosynchronous orbit (GEO) is 36,000 kilometres high – three times the diameter of the whole Earth. An elliptical orbit (EO) can 'corkscrew' around the world – the apogee is the furthest point from Earth and the perigee is the nearest point.

Types of orbit

Low Earth orbit   The Space Shuttle and most other launchers take their payloads into low Earth orbit (LEO). This is roughly circular, between 150–500 kilometres above the Earth and the usual orbit for spacecraft.

Elliptical orbit   Many survey satellites need to be close to Earth, to get a good view. If a satellite tried to orbit Earth in a circular path at a low height, it would be pulled back by gravity. The lop-sided, elliptical orbit (EO) swings far away from the planet (the apogee of the orbit) and then comes in close (the perigee) for surveying (see the diagram above).

Geosynchronous orbit   Many comsats and navsats (navigation satellites) boost to a very wide circular orbit 36,000 kilometres from Earth. The satellite speeds along at 11,000 kph. But the planet below is also turning, and the two speeds match. From Earth's surface, the satellite seems to stay in the same place.

The life of a satellite

No satellite lasts for ever. Like any delicate and complicated machine, it may break down. This happened especially with early satellites, whose electronic circuits were less reliable. Solar panels and batteries become less efficient. Manoeuvring jets or thrusters run out of 'puff'. A satellite may even get hit by a meteoroid, and smashed and destroyed.

Mending satellites

Some broken satellites can be repaired. Astronauts manoeuvre their spacecraft close to the satellite, as both speed along at 27,000 kph. The spacesuited astronauts leave their craft, taking tools and spare parts with them, to work outside. This is very difficult. During each orbit, they go from great heat and glare on the sunny side of Earth, to the cold, dark, shaded side. Tools and parts must be fixed down, or they float away into space. And the astronaut must know how the satellite works and how to mend it. If the new part is the wrong one, the spare is a long way below.

In the Space Shuttle, a satellite can be grabbed and pulled into the cargo bay. The astronauts repair the satellite here, where conditions are easier. Or the Shuttle can bring the satellite back to Earth. However, only satellites in low orbits can be repaired or recovered by astronauts. Those in higher orbits cannot be reached by the usual manned spacecraft.

It took five space-walks to repair the *Hubble Space Telescope* satellite (see page 37). Here, it is manoeuvred into the Space Shuttle's open payload bay.

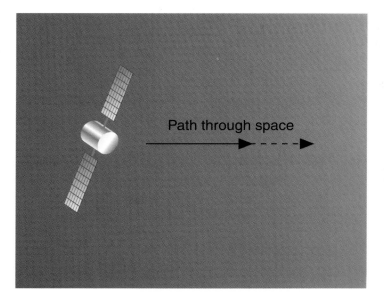

Any object goes straight at the same speed, unless forces act on it. In deep space, there are no forces.

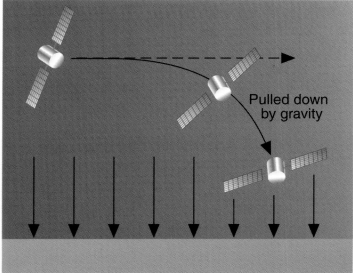

Near Earth, the satellite tries to go straight. But Earth's gravity pulls it down towards the surface.

How do satellites stay up?

When a satellite is launched, it must be given a certain amount of forward speed. There is no air in space and therefore nothing to resist its progress, so the satellite does not slow down. It tries to go straight, in accordance with a basic law of motion, but the gravity of the Earth exerts a downward pull. If the satellite is travelling at a certain speed, it does not fall back to Earth but begins to follow a curved path, or orbit. Different satellite speeds give different orbits.

- At less than 27,000 kph, the satellite falls back to Earth.
- At 27,000 kph, the satellite stays in circular orbit.
- At 27,000–36,000 kph, the satellite goes into elliptical orbit.
- At more than 36,000 kph, the satellite flies off into space.

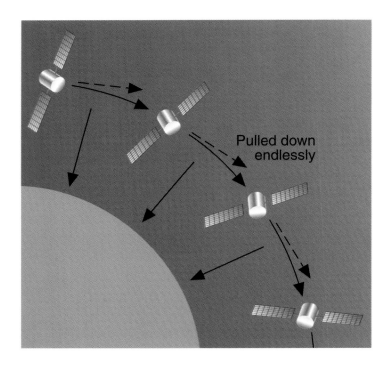

Earth is curved, so the satellite follows the curve. It orbits, endlessly 'falling' but never getting lower.

COMMUNICATION SATELLITES

A comsat orbits far above the planet, keeping its dish antennae pointed at Earth and its solar panels facing the Sun. The gold foil 'cloak' keeps out harmful radiation and micro-meteorites.

Satellites are changing modern life almost every month – and especially the way we send information and communicate with each other.

Satellites in the system

You win a huge prize on the national lottery, and you want to tell your aunt, who lives on the other side of the world. You pick up the telephone and dial her number. A few seconds later you are chatting with her, over a distance of 20,000 kilometres. How? By satellite.

The sound waves of your voice are converted to electrical signals in the telephone, and sent along telephone wires to the local exchange. Here they may be converted to pulses of laser light that flash along a main fibre-optic cable, to a larger telephone exchange. This changes the light signals to microwaves, which are beamed across the landscape to the nearest satellite ground station.

Up-link

At the ground station, the signals change from microwaves back to electricity. Then they are converted to radio waves or microwaves and transmitted or sent out, beamed up into the sky by a large antenna. The radio signals go into space, aimed exactly at a comsat in geosynchronous orbit, 36,000 kilometres away. (This is a very long distance, since the entire Earth is 12,750 kilometres across.) This is the up-link.

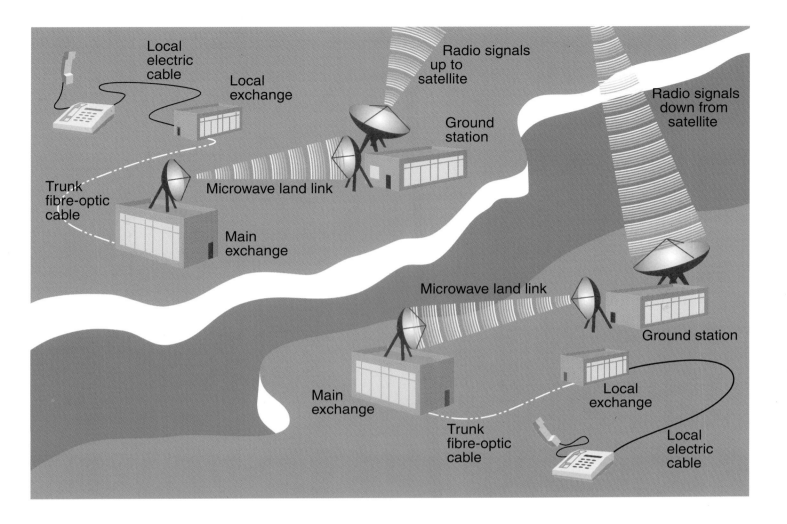

Local electric cable

Local exchange

Radio signals up to satellite

Ground station

Trunk fibre-optic cable

Microwave land link

Main exchange

Radio signals down from satellite

Microwave land link

Ground station

Main exchange

Trunk fibre-optic cable

Local exchange

Local electric cable

Down-link

The comsat's antenna collects the waves, and the receiver turns them into electrical signals. They are strengthened or boosted by amplifiers, changed back into waves and sent out again by the comsat's own transmitter. The waves are aimed back to Earth, and received by a large dish antenna at the ground station thousands of kilometres away. This is the down-link. The waves are changed back to electrical signals at the receiving ground station, and the whole process is reversed. They become microwaves, then laser light pulses, then electrical signals again at the local telephone exchange. Finally, they change back to sound waves, which your aunt hears from her telephone's earpiece. Thanks to the comsat, the whole process takes less than half a second, and your aunt sounds as clear as if she is in the next room.

The sound of your voice is changed into electrical signals, light pulses, microwaves and radio waves, then sent via satellite to the receiving ground station in another country where the whole process is reversed.

What do comsats communicate?

The most obvious use of comsats is for radio signals, which represent sounds and images – telephone conversations and television programmes. But the signals can represent many other forms of information. They could be from fax machines, telex machines or computers communicating by modems. It could be a news story and photographs being sent by a journalist, direct to a newspaper on the other side of the world, for immediate printing.

A modern international company uses huge amounts of computing power, and many satellite channels to send and receive information between its different offices.

Business and finance

In fact, much of the 'traffic' handled by a modern comsat is not ordinary people on the telephone, or television programmes. It is information being transferred between computers in the offices of large international companies or institutions around the world. These include banks, insurance companies, manufacturers and retailers, and also government departments. The information may concern their finances and business dealings, reports and letters, stocks and shares or sales and accounts. It is usually encrypted (put into a special code), to prevent other people 'listening in' and finding out secrets.

In touch in remote areas

Satellites are very useful for communication in remote areas. In the huge open spaces of northern North America, northern Asia, North Africa, central Australia and southern South America, it is almost impossible to connect every house or dwelling by a telephone line. It is the same on remote ocean islands. Ordinary mobile telephone networks do not stretch so far, and they can be blocked by high mountains. So local ground stations provide satellite links into the main telecommunications network. Satellites keep people in these faraway places in touch with the rest of the world.

Above **In the Middle East deserts, an oil worker sets up a white, square-framed satellite dish and a silver box of electronic equipment. He can talk via the Inmarsat satellite system to anyone, anywhere.**

Ground stations

Satellite ground (or earth) stations are vital links between the Earth's surface and satellites thousands of kilometres above. Their large dish or rod antennae can transmit and receive. Transmitters focus radio or microwave signals into a narrow and powerful beam, which the satellite receives clearly. Receiving dishes gather or collect weak waves from the satellite and focus them into a stronger beam for the receiver unit. The dishes can be swivelled precisely by large computer-controlled electric motors, to follow (or track) a satellite that moves overhead.

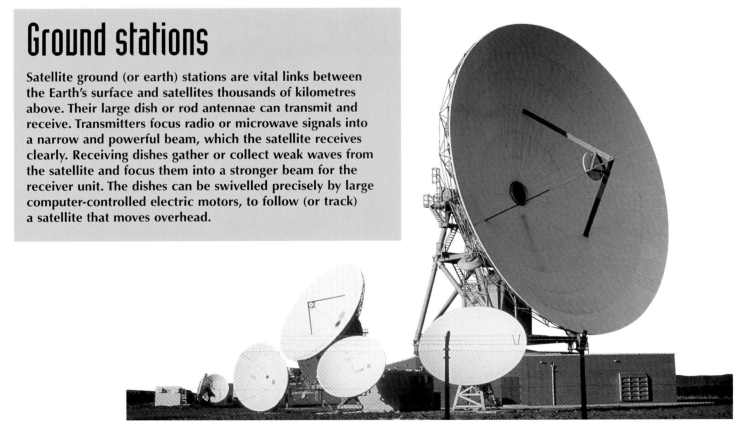

Satellite TV

Satellites have played a part in certain television broadcasts since the 1960s. The programmes were mainly live news reports or sports link-ups with countries all round the globe.

Watching a satellite channel – the television signals are beamed from a comsat 36,000 kilometres away in space, direct into homes.

DBS systems

When we talk about satellite television nowadays, we usually mean DBS (direct broadcast satellite) systems. In this case, the signals come from the satellite in geosynchronous orbit, directly to each viewer. In other words, the down-link is straight into the home. The signals are received by a small dish antenna – the domestic 'satellite dish'. A satellite of the DBS system must have a powerful transmitter. Its signals are not aimed at one ground station. They spread over a huge area, called the satellite's footprint. They must be strong enough to be received by a dish that is cheap to buy, and small enough to install in almost any home.

Pay as you watch

Anyone with a suitable dish could receive satellite television 'free'. How do the satellite operators make any profit? They scramble their signals into a code. Then they sell decoder units worked by paycards, to unscramble the signals again. The scrambling system changes regularly, so that new paycards are always needed.

More and more channels

Satellite television is a very complicated and fast-growing business. Most dishes in Europe point at the Astra series of geostationary satellites, launched from 1990. These are operated by a company called ESS (European Satellite Society), based in Luxemburg. Various television companies, such as Sky, rent channels on the Astra satellites and broadcast programmes from them.

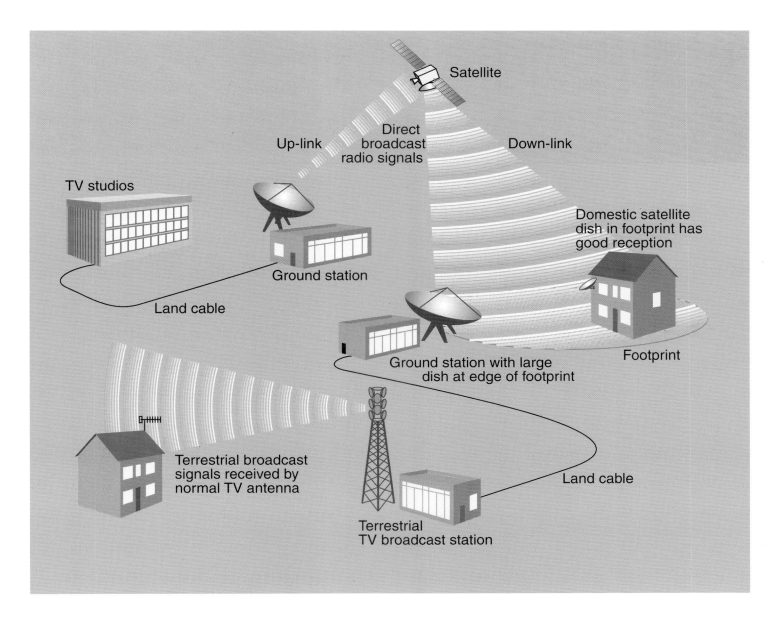

Satellite

Up-link

Direct broadcast radio signals

Down-link

TV studios

Ground station

Land cable

Domestic satellite dish in footprint has good reception

Ground station with large dish at edge of footprint

Footprint

Terrestrial broadcast signals received by normal TV antenna

Terrestrial TV broadcast station

Land cable

From the mid 1990s, another series of satellites, known as Hot Birds, are providing DBS in Europe. Hot Birds are more powerful than Astras, offering clearer television pictures. They can transmit signals in digital form, which will be used in future for the bigger and better pictures of HDTV (high-definition television), as well as in the usual analogue signals. Hot Birds will cover a wide area, from Ireland in the west, across Europe to the Ukraine in the east.

DBS is developing in this complicated and competitive way, in many regions around the world. Eventually, satellite television could provide hundreds of channels. But who will make and watch all the programmes, and will they be any good?

There are several ways to send and receive the radio signals that represent television programmes. DBS goes straight to individual receiver dishes. Indirect systems go to ground-based or terrestrial systems for local broadcast.

Satellites to the rescue

This radio outside broadcast truck is, in effect, a mobile satellite ground station. The large dish antenna unfolds and points accurately at a comsat, to create an up-link.

It is a quiet day in a remote town, nestled among the mountains. People are shopping, drinking spiced tea and chatting in the sunshine. Suddenly, they stop and listen to a distant rumble. The ground seems to lurch and shake. Cups fall off tables. The rocking gets worse. Windows crash from their frames, walls crack and buildings begin to sway and topple. An earthquake has struck.

Detected by satellite

An hour later, the town is in ruins. Electricity and telephone lines are down. Roads and railway lines are destroyed. The local radio–television station is devastated. All links with the outside world are cut.

A survey satellite, passing overhead, has photographed the destruction. Its ground computer compares the new picture with the pictures already in its memory banks. It detects the largescale changes in the buildings and landscape and flashes a warning to the satellite monitoring staff. They check the pictures and alert the world's emergency and rescue services, which swing into action.

Helicopters arrive at the scene, carrying medical staff, search-and-rescue teams and satellite communications experts with film crews and news reporters. The satellite experts unfold their dish-shaped antenna. Using a magnetic compass and a sextant, they point it at their comsat. The operators divert some of its normal 'traffic' of everyday telephone calls and television programmes, to create free channels just for the emergency. Up- and down-links are quickly established.

World coverage, world action

Within two hours, rescue experts are sending information about the scale of the destruction to international agencies, via the priority satellite links. As television news crews point their cameras at the rubble and interview rescued victims, the world watches. The pictures are sent from the news camera on a short radio link to the temporary satellite dish, which is the ground station. This transmits them up to the satellite, which beams them to receiving stations in its 'footprint'. Via more up- and down-links, the pictures are spread around the globe, to national and regional television stations.

The dreadful news of the earthquake creates great interest and people in many countries want to help. Within a day, charities have begun to collect money, clothes, preserved foods, blankets, tents and other essential items. Rescue workers and aid volunteers are arriving in the town. The lives of the victims are being saved, and their suffering eased. Without satellites, the outside world may not yet even know about the great disaster.

A severe earthquake destroys all normal methods of transport and communications, such as roads, railways and telephone lines. However, satellite communications are unaffected.

SATELLITE NAVIGATION

Have you ever been on a long sea voyage? A few hours away from land, you lose track of your direction, and even the time. Of course, the Sun rises and sets, and the Moon and stars move in regular patterns across the night sky. But what if it is cloudy or foggy? You can use your magnetic compass, which points to the North Pole. But this shows your direction only, not your position. Are winds and tides pushing you off course?

Ferdinand Magellan used traditional navigation for the first round-the-world voyage, 1519–22. Sadly he was killed in what is now the Philippines, but his shipmates completed the journey.

Replacing the compass?

Sailors, pilots and other long-distance travellers are well trained in finding their position and direction using traditional methods such as the compass and sextant. Overland explorers and surveyors use similar techniques. But satellite navigation is changing all this – and fast. Navsats have been helping crews of ships and large planes for more than twenty years. Many of them work using the Doppler effect (see panel opposite).

Nowadays, all large ships and planes carry navsat equipment. It generally works using the satellites of the GPS (global positioning system), described on page 26. The equipment is fully automatic and computerized. However, it can be disturbed by electrical storms, power or computer failure, so crews still have their compass and sextant standing by.

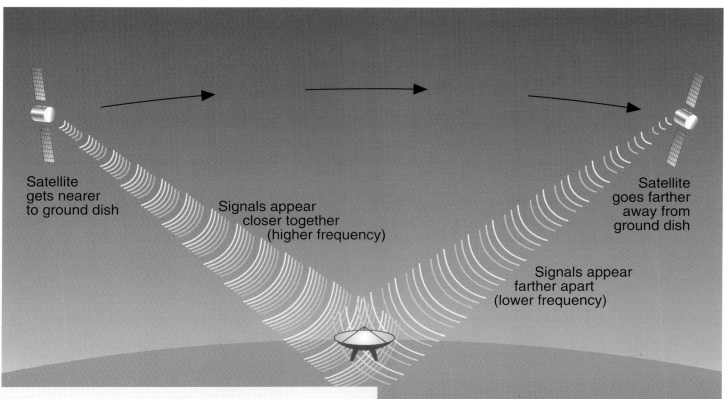

Satellite gets nearer to ground dish

Signals appear closer together (higher frequency)

Satellite goes farther away from ground dish

Signals appear farther apart (lower frequency)

The Doppler effect

NIAAOOOW! A motorcycle whizzes past, and its engine whine seems to go from high to low. But the rider knows that the engine pitch is unchanged. This is the Doppler effect, discovered by Austrian physicist Christian Doppler (1803–53). The motorcycle engine sends out regular sound waves. Coming towards you, the waves are squashed together, giving a higher frequency or shriller pitch. Similarly, going away from you, the waves are stretched out to give a lower frequency or deeper pitch.

The Doppler effect also works with radio waves. As a satellite in orbit approaches you, the signals from its pulse-producing oscillator seem closer together. The reverse happens after it has passed overhead. Sensitive electrical equipment detects this change. Compare the Doppler effect of signals from several satellites, whose orbits you know exactly, and you can calculate your position on Earth.

The flight deck computer screens of a modern jetliner show exact position, heading, groundspeed and airspeed, all with the help of navsats.

Never lost again

A new gadget is appearing on the satellite navigation scene. It looks like a mobile phone. In fact, it is a receiver for radio signals from satellites. It can show your position or location anywhere in the world, to within 100 metres. It uses the satellites of the GPS. With one of these devices, you need never get lost again.

This car driver presses the buttons on her GPS device, and receives a read-out of her position. She can then plot this on to a map.

The satellite system of the GPS is known as NAVSTAR (navigation system using time and ranging). Anyone with suitable equipment is free to use it. The system uses a network of twenty-one satellites in specialized orbits around the Earth. Each satellite has its own very accurate atomic clocks. It sends out codes of radio signals which carry the satellite's own identification or 'name', its exact position in orbit (since the orbits are known to incredible accuracy), and the precise time.

Where are you now?

The typical navsat receiver has a small antenna that picks up signals direct from the satellites. At any time and place, there could be six or more signals coming in, strong enough to be received clearly. The times will be slightly different, since the signals take different lengths of time to reach the receiver, depending on the receiver's distance from the satellite. A small computer in the receiver compares these times, calculates the differences and converts them to a display showing the receiver's location. If you are moving, such as in a car, the system also shows your direction, or heading, and your speed.

The real-time map

Some navsat receivers have plug-in chips or cartridges which contain, in computer memory form, a map of the region. It has roads, railways, hills, coastlines, islands and other features. The device can then plot your position and route directly on to the map and display the results. This allows the system to show your height above sea level, which is very useful if you are walking or driving through hilly or mountainous areas. As you travel along, you can see yourself as a 'blip' on the small display screen, moving through the countryside.

International rescue

SARSAT (search and rescue satellite) is the name for a system which can locate people in distress, in planes, boats or land vehicles, so that they can be rescued. SARSAT uses emergency channels on various communication, navigation and other satellites. If you suffer a power failure, a water leakage or a fire, for example, your special battery-powered SARSAT transmitter automatically switches on. Its international signal is picked up by the satellites and sent back to ground stations, to tell them about the emergency and your location. SARSAT is go!

WEATHER AND SURVEYING SATELLITES

Is the weather forecast really more accurate than it was before weather satellites? The answer is probably, 'yes'. Nowadays, at least, we can see satellite pictures, to prove that stormclouds have swept over the region.

The weather forecast on television and radio, and in the newspapers, is just one small part of a vast and complicated business involving satellites, weather experts and thousands of other people all around the planet. Some of the world's biggest computers handle the incredible amounts of information, and try to predict weather patterns. Many people rely on the forecasts, including pilots, ships' captains, fishing fleets, farmers and hillwalkers.

The weather forecast is an end-product of information collected by hundreds of weather stations, dozens of satellites and weather balloons and planes.

Watching the weather

There are hundreds of satellites involved in meteorology, which is the study of the Earth's atmosphere, and especially its weather and climate. Weather happens over the shorter time of days and weeks, while climate is long term, over years and centuries. Weather satellites or meteosats usually gather information of many kinds, not just about clouds and rain. They may also act as survsats (see page 30).

As well as cameras, weather satellites carry radiometers, which measure the temperature at different levels in the atmosphere. They can even detect the temperature of the sea's surface and identify snow and ice, to help ships avoid these areas.

Nimbus 7

In 1978, *Nimbus 7* became the first satellite designed specially to check the atmosphere for polluting substances and the changes they cause, such as the 'ozone hole', the greenhouse effect and global warming. The information gathered by *Nimbus 7* and later satellites has prompted worldwide campaigns to reduce pollution and clean up the environment.

What meteosats show about weather

Meteosat information is especially important where there are few weather stations on the ground, such as in deserts, rainforests and polar regions. The information from cameras and sensors on the dozens of meteosats now in orbit, is combined to produce a detailed picture of weather and conditions all over the world. This includes:

- cloud cover,
- rainfall,
- storms, typhoons and hurricanes,
- mist and fog,
- snow and ice on land,
- sea ice and snow,
- temperature at the sea's surface,
- temperatures at different heights in the atmosphere.

Orbiting cameras

Survsats are probably photographing the area where you live, right now. No place on Earth remains hidden from the cameras of these land and sea observation satellites. They take normal photographs of Earth, giving the view that you would see from the satellite, but they also take other kinds of photograph. Visible light rays are only a tiny part of a whole range or spectrum of waves, called the electromagnetic spectrum. This includes infra-red or heat rays, ultraviolet (UV) rays, microwaves, radio waves, X-rays and many others (see panel).

This *SPOT-1* satellite photograph was taken not with light, but with infra-red waves. Greens become reds, showing fields of crops at different stages of growth. To the left is the Detroit River, and upper left is the city of Detroit, USA.

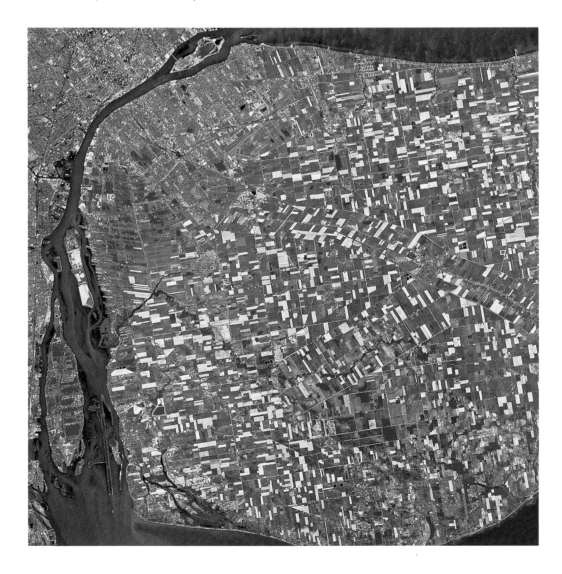

Light, radio and the EMS

Light rays or waves are part of a whole range of waves, called the electromagnetic spectrum (EMS). This includes radio waves, microwaves, infra-red or heat rays, ordinary light rays, ultraviolet (UV) rays, X-rays and gamma rays.

The waves of the EMS are all basically the same form of energy. They differ only in size or wavelength – the distance from the peak of one wave to the peak of the next. Radio waves have a wavelength of about 1 to 1,000 metres, while microwaves are between 1 centimetre and 1 metre long. The wavelengths of light rays are so short that you could pack more than 1,000 into 1 millimetre.

Because the waves of the EMS are all essentially the same, they all travel at the same speed – about 300,000 kilometres per second – commonly known as the speed of light. Satellites use radio waves, and since these waves travel so fast, satellites are able to receive and transmit information almost instantly.

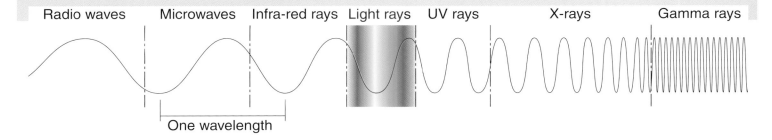

Radio waves   Microwaves   Infra-red rays   Light rays   UV rays   X-rays   Gamma rays

One wavelength

A line of photographs

Survsat cameras record these different waves. As they orbit, they take pictures one after the other, in a line or transect. The results are sent back to Earth as radio signals. The pictures might cover an area of thousands of square kilometres, or just a few hectares, depending on the 'telescope' power of the camera. They can be joined into one large picture that covers a continent and reveals far more than we could see with our own eyes.

What can they detect?

Survsat information is fed through computers to produce clearer or enhanced pictures. The images of different types of waves are compared. This is the science of remote sensing. From the results, we can tell the difference, not only between land and water, but also between built-up towns and rural countryside, between different types of crops in the fields or trees in the forest, and even between crops that are growing well and those suffering disease or drought.

How survsats are used

People can receive information direct from a survsat if they have suitable equipment. Or they can buy pictures and reports from agencies. The information is used in many different ways. One important use is to check and update maps, and to make new maps of remote regions that have never been accurately surveyed.

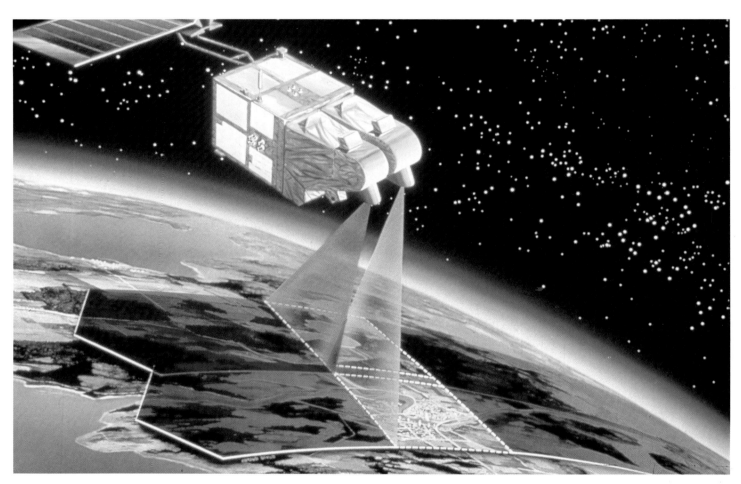

Images from such satellites as the French survsat, *SPOT-1*, help land-based surveyors to show which areas of land are best for farming various crops, where to obtain water for them, and whether there might be oil, metals and minerals under the surface.

The computer can add or change colours, for example, to show different types of rocks. Ranchers and foresters can check vast areas by looking at them in a photograph, rather than flying or driving for hours. Governments can see how much land in their country is set aside for growing crops, and how much food is being produced. They can also find people who are claiming farm grants and subsidies, logging trees or digging mines – against the law.

Seasat

Seasat (sea satellite) was launched on 26 June 1978 to study the Earth's main lakes, seas and oceans, but it broke down about four months later. However, it tested various devices which could measure oil pollution, wave heights to within a metre, wind speeds to within 2 metres per second, water temperature, the rate of falling rain, the movement of sea ice and even the ice's age. Better versions of these devices have been used since on many other satellites.

Satellite radar

Not all the radio signals from a satellite reach the Earth's surface. Satellite radar sends out radio signals from a transmitter, which are reflected back off objects such as clouds, rain, aircraft, ships and tall buildings. (Ships and planes have similar radar systems.) The satellite's radar receiver picks up the radio 'echoes', and their signals are sent on the down-link in the usual way.

The rainfall picture on the weather forecast is usually obtained by satellite radar. A satellite's own altitude radar can detect its height above the Earth to within 10 cm.

A global map of wind speeds using information from NASA's seasat.

Research satellites

Above **COBE was built at USA's main ground station, the Goddard Space Flight Center at Greenbelt, near Washington, DC.**

Some satellites do not look down at Earth. They look away into deep space, and at the Moon, Sun, planets, stars and galaxies. They are research satellites, designed by scientists to detect all kinds of rays, waves and particles coming through space. Optical (light) and radio telescopes on the Earth's surface also do this. But the scattering effects of air and dust in the atmosphere make their images blurred. In space, there is almost nothing to weaken or distort the rays and particles.

A combination photograph of our own galaxy, sometimes called the Milky Way, taken by the COBE satellite using infra-red rays.

The tasks of research satellites are mostly 'pure research' – finding knowledge for its own sake, to increase our understanding of the universe. If the information turns out to be useful in some way, it is called 'applied research'. Mostly, it has little effect on daily life, except for the science we learn at school, and for the jobs of millions of career scientists. But one day, a satellite may detect signals from alien beings out in space, or even one of their spacecraft. Then we would all hear about it. Or would we?

COBE

The *COBE* (*Cosmic Background Explorer*) satellite hit the news in May 1992. Using its microwave and other sensors, scientists announced they had detected ripples of matter, or a background of rays and radiation, that was the same all over the universe. They suggested that it was left over from when time began and the universe came into being – 'echoes of the Big Bang'.

IRAS

IRAS (US-Dutch *Infra-red Astronomical Satellite*) has changed our view of the universe. Through a normal light telescope, huge areas of space look black and empty. But during its active life in 1983, *IRAS's* telescope saw infra-red rays. It showed huge numbers of galaxies in the gaps, sending out infra-red, but no visible light rays. This means the universe could contain much more matter than once believed. The European Space Agency plans to launch a new satellite, *ISO* (*Infra-red Space Observatory*), in the 1990s.

IRAS in its near-polar orbit, 900 kilometres high, circling Earth fourteen times daily. The opening or aperture of its infra-red telescope is 60 centimetres across.

IUE

Launched in 1978, *IUE* (*International Ultraviolet Explorer*) has far outlived its original active life. It was due to 'retire' in 1982, but parts of it are still working. It has picked up ultraviolet rays from thousands of immense and mysterious deep-space bodies such collapsing stars, nebulas and quasars. In the 1990s, NASA's *EUE* (*Extreme Ultraviolet Explorer*) took over its job and discovered the hottest stars in our part of the universe.

Uhuru, Exosat and Rosat

If you could see X-rays, the night sky would be very bright indeed, with millions of stars and other objects sending them out. *Uhuru* (1970–79) was the first satellite designed specially to detect X-rays. It was followed by *Exosat* (1983–86) and then *Rosat* (launched 1990). This last satellite is named after Wilhelm Roentgen (1845–1923), who discovered X-rays in 1895.

Uhuru, also called *Explorer 42*, was a fairly small satellite. Its X-ray detector is behind the black rectangle (top left) and its solar panels are top right.

Hubble Space Telescope

Named after US astronomer Edwin Hubble (1889–1953), this satellite is an orbiting telescope. It was launched in 1990 with the hope of incredibly clear pictures of space, since it was far above the fuzziness of our atmosphere. But the shape of the telescope's reflecting mirror was wrong, and its images were blurred. In December 1993 astronauts from the Space Shuttle *Endeavour* fixed a new camera to it while in orbit, and mostly solved the problem.

SETI project

The rays and pulses that satellites pick up from space are constantly being studied for possible signals from aliens. Such signals would be non-random, and have some order or pattern imposed on them. This is part of the worldwide and ongoing SETI project, the Search for Extra-Terrestrial Intelligence.

Organizing satellites

Why don't satellites crash into each other? Why don't their radio signals interfere with each other? What happens if a satellite goes wrong and falls back to Earth, causing damage or even death? International and national groups co-operate to organize the use of space. They sign agreements, laws and treaties. Anyone planning to launch a satellite has a selection of vacant orbits and radio frequencies for general use. Some radio channels are always kept open and reserved for emergency use only.

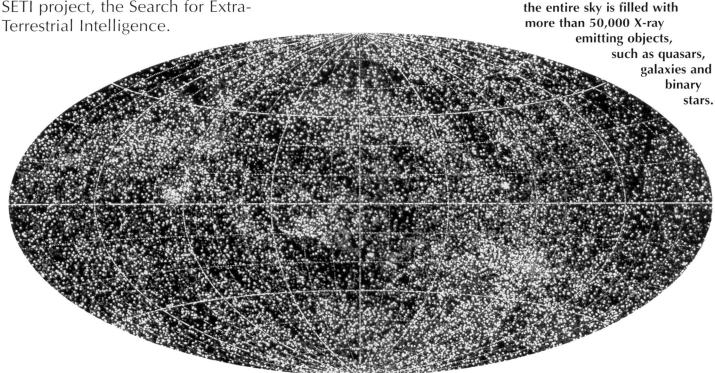

Rosat's photographs show the entire sky is filled with more than 50,000 X-ray emitting objects, such as quasars, galaxies and binary stars.

MILITARY AND SECRET SATELLITES

S pysats (spy satellites) are orbiting over us, day and night. They can see the Earth's surface with incredibly powerful telescopes. They photograph objects as small as cars and perhaps even individual people. They watch war zones and areas of unrest for the movements of troops, tanks, air force planes and navy ships. They 'listen in' to radio broadcasts on Earth and to the radio information being sent via other satellites. This is part of the eavesdropping known as electronic surveillance, and is done by satellites called 'ferrets'.

Many satellites can locate atomic, nuclear or other explosions. They can also detect rocket and missile launches, and track their paths. But how do we know all this, if these 'orbiting spies' are supposed to be secret?

No-longer-secret satellites

Much of the information about older spysats has been made available by the nations which operated them. For example, from 1962, the former USSR launched about 100 satellites each year, under the Cosmos programme, whose missions were not clear. It is now known that many of them were used for reconnaissance and military purposes.

Since the break-up of the USSR, the Soviet Cosmos satellites are operated by Russia and the CIS.

On 5 April 1995 an Israeli satellite *Ofeq-3* was launched. Experts calculate that its orbit takes it over the Middle East region six times during each daylight period, at altitudes as low as 365 kilometres. With modern cameras, it could make out objects on the ground smaller than 2 metres. But like hundreds of other spysats launched by dozens of different nations, governments say nothing official.

Evidence in pictures

Occasionally, a satellite photograph is released by a spying government to the newspapers and television. It might show evidence of military build-ups, or war crimes and atrocities. For example, the photograph could reveal tanks massing in an area that is supposed to be neutral, or freshly disturbed earth marking mass graves. By this method a government can create public pressure around the world to discourage another government from war or human rights violations.

Spysats also have non-military purposes. Their equipment is similar to many survey and observation satellites, so they can help to detect activities which are against the law. These include pollution, cutting down trees in nature reserves and protected forests, and illegal burning or mining.

South American rainforest has been cut down in the area of the Rio San Francisco, Brazil. Satellite photos help to show if clearance is within the law.

Satellites and wars

An entire city is photographed by a satellite 700 kilometres above. Large-scale movements of planes, ships or tanks show at once. This is Kuwait City two weeks after invasion by Iraqi forces, during the Gulf Conflict of 1990–91.

Satellites are also used for military navigation, so that troops, ships, planes, military vehicles, missiles and rockets know exactly where they are, and where they are heading. This means missiles can be aimed with pinpoint accuracy.

The GPS system (see page 26) was set up mainly for the US military. Anyone can use it, but GPS satellites broadcast two types of signals. One is for general civilian use, and it allows a location 'fix' to within 100 metres, and sometimes to 50 metres. The second signal is encrypted, or scrambled into a special code. Only the US armed forces know the code, and it allows them to fix a position to an accuracy of 10 metres or less.

The spying game

Modern-day warfare owes much to information that one side knows about the other side, which can only have been obtained from satellites. This includes detailed knowledge of the enemy's armed forces. For example, if you are a military commander, you know from satellite information that the enemy plans to attack a certain area. So you can then move your troops to defend it, and perhaps make an unexpected attack elsewhere.

During the Gulf War in 1990–91, satellites were used to spy on Iraqi troops, tanks and planes, to guide missiles to their targets, to assess the damage caused by bombs and missiles, and to assist troops on secret missions in enemy territory.

The 'Star Wars' programme

'Star Wars' was the popular name for the USA's SDI (Strategic Defence Initiative), that was planned from 1983. The idea was to put dozens of satellites in orbit to cover the whole Earth. They would detect the heat from enemy rockets and missiles, in case of attack. The missiles would be destroyed by powerful laser beams, X-rays and particle beams, some fired from the ground and others from satellites.

Various SDI satellites and other equipment were tested, but the US government decided to cut back the project to a much smaller one. There were several reasons for this, such as the gigantic costs involved, the break-up of the USA's main rival – the USSR – as well as technical problems concerning the satellites, their weapons, and the immense computing power needed to control them.

Satellites and space stations blast enemy missiles with laser beams, in this 1980s artist's view of 'Star Wars' – the USA's plan to defend itself against missile attack.

SATELLITES IN THE FUTURE

Every part of the satellite business is powering ahead. Many countries are developing rockets and less expensive ways of launching satellites. Hundreds are put into orbit each year, and there are huge profits to be made.

What's the weather like in Butte, Montana, USA? Anyone can find out using the Internet system of computers joined by telephone lines that use satellite links.

Even more TV channels

Satellites will continue to bring many changes to our daily lives. Future comsats will carry even more television and telephone channels, making it easier and cheaper to make long-distance calls, and to link into computer modems, e-mail and Internet systems. They will also allow us to receive yet more television channels – perhaps hundreds. Satellites will be a vital part of the Information Revolution of the twenty-first century.

Knowing your place

Future mobile telephones will be fitted with GPS navigation. With this equipment, you will be able to find your location anywhere in the world, tell your friends on the phone, and meet them at exactly the right time and place – even in a thick wood or at sea. The equipment might be linked to a car, so that if you take a wrong turn, a warning sounds.

Satellites are becoming more powerful, so they can send out stronger radio waves. These can be detected by smaller antennae and receivers. Satellite dishes will become smaller, fitted to cars and even to personal television-video-stereo sets. Eventually, the equipment might fit into a wristwatch.

Birthplace of a thousand stars: a gigantic pillar of gas rears from the Eagle Nebula, 66,000 million million kilometres away in deepest space. The *Hubble Space Telescope* takes such awesome pictures almost every week.

Weather to war

Will the weather forecast ever be right all the time? More meteosat information, combined with better computer programmes to mimic the weather, should make short-term forecasts more accurate. But the long-term outlook is, as usual, changeable.

Could satellite surveillance ultimately prevent war and conflict? It seems that however science and technology progress, some people will always want to wage wars. Satellites simply become another tool or weapon in the battle. The Gulf War showed that satellites were not as useful as people had hoped, and that tanks and warplanes were easily hidden from them.

The on-going development of satellite technology adds immensely to scientific knowledge. It also has spin-offs in daily life, such as better computers and electronic equipment. Research satellites, meanwhile, are helping us to discover the secrets of deep space. One day, a satellite may reveal the answer to life, the universe and everything.

DATE CHART

1903 Russian schoolteacher Konstantin Tsiolkovsky begins the modern science of rocketry by suggesting that a very powerful rocket could escape the gravity of the Earth and reach space – the first scientific proposal that space travel is possible.

1926 American scientist Robert Goddard launches the first modern-style, liquid-fuel rocket. It travels just 56 metres, but opens the way for more powerful rockets that can reach space.

1945 Scientist and writer Arthur C. Clark suggests that satellites could carry out global communications and proposes the geostationary orbit for 'satellite repeaters'.

1957 On 4 October the world's first satellite *Sputnik 1* (the name means 'travelling companion') is launched by a Soviet A rocket from Baikonaur Cosmodrome in Kazakhstan, beginning the Space Age.

On 3 November *Sputnik 2* carries the first living thing into space – a dog, Laika. She survives for several days, showing life is possible inside a spacecraft.

1958 On 31 January the USA launches its first satellite, *Explorer 1*, from Cape Canaveral, Florida.

1960 The USA launches the first weather satellite or meteosat *TIROS 1* (*Television and Infra-red Observation Satellite*) on 1 April.

1961 A Vostok spacecraft (based on Sputnik designs) becomes the first manned satellite as it carried the first space person, Russian cosmonaut Yuri Gagarin, on one orbit of the Earth.

1962 *Telstar 1* is launched on 10 July by a Delta rocket from the US space base of Cape Canaveral and relays radio signals for the first live transatlantic television broadcasts.

1963 Launched on 8 May, *Telstar 2* relays radio signals for the first live transatlantic television broadcasts in colour.

1964 Twelve nations form Intelsat (International Telecommunications Satellite Organization), to develop a global communications network.

The Transit system of satellites begins the first major service for satellite navigation.

1965 Intelsat launches *Intelsat 1*, nicknamed *Early Bird*, the first commercial comsat in geosynchronous orbit.

Also in 1965, France becomes the third nation in space with the launch of the satellite *A-1* from a French military base at Hammaguir in the Sahara Desert, North Africa.

1970 Japan becomes the fourth nation in space with the launch of its *Osumi* satellite, and China follows with the *China 1* satellite.

1971 The UK becomes the sixth space nation with the satellite *Prospero*, launched from the Woomera Base in the Australian outback by a *Black Arrow* rocket.

Intelsat begins the launches of its *Intelsat IVs* into geosynchronous orbits above the Atlantic, Indian and Pacific Oceans, to cover most of the inhabited globe.

1974 The USA's landsat series begins in July, photographing the Earth's surface for mapping and surveys.

1975 On 16 October the USA's NOAA (National Oceanographic and Atmospheric Administration) launches the first *GOES* (*Geostationary Operational Environmental Satellite*), a major series of meteosats.

1980 USA, USSR, France and Canada set up SARSAT (search and rescue satellite) to locate people in distress in planes, boats or land vehicles, for international rescue.

1983 On its fifth mission the US Space Shuttle launches two commercial comsats into Earth orbit.

The European launcher *Ariane 1* successfully puts its first two satellites into orbit.

1986 The US Space Shuttle *Challenger* explodes just after lift-off, causing postponement of the Shuttle programme.

1990 Launches begin of the Astra series of geostationary satellites, for DBS (direct-broadcast satellite television).

1990 Launch of the *Hubble Space Telescope*.

1992 Information from the *COBE* (*Cosmic Background Explorer*) satellite launched by NASA in 1989 leads scientists to announce detection of ripples of background matter and radiation – 'echoes of the Big Bang'.

1993 The final satellite takes its place to complete the NAVSTAR network for GPS (global positioning system) for satellite navigation.

1995 Eutelsat plans launches of its Hot Bird satellites for broadcast of digital signals for HDTV (high-definition television).

GLOSSARY

analogue Using a physical quantity, such as volts of electricity, to represent different kinds of information.

atomic clocks Extremely accurate clocks that count time by the incredibly fast vibrations of atoms.

attitude The position of a satellite and the direction it faces, especially in relation to the Earth and Sun.

Big Bang The immense cosmic explosion that, according to many scientists, brought the universe into existence about 15,000 million years ago.

digital Using digits or numbers to represent different kinds of information.

e-mail Electronic mail. The process of sending messages and information between computers using modems.

fibre-optic cable A communications cable containing many hair-thin strands of special glass (optical fibres). It carries information as pulses of laser light.

infra-red Waves of the electromagnetic spectrum that are longer than the longest or red waves of visible light. We cannot see them, but we can feel them as heat.

Internet The international network of computers connected by modems and phone lines that, in theory, forms a vast global web of electronic communication.

launch vehicle A vehicle that carries satellites, spacecraft and other objects into space – what many people call a 'rocket'.

meteoroid A rocky or metallic object that travels through space, usually in orbit around the Sun. It may enter and burn up in the Earth's atmosphere as a meteor or 'shooting star', or fall to the surface as a meteorite.

microwaves Waves of the electromagnetic spectrum. We cannot see them, but we can use them, for example, to generate heat, as in a microwave oven.

modem A device that changes information in a computer from electrical pulses into pulses that can be sent along telephone lines, allowing computers to talk to each other.

payload An object, such as a satellite, carried by a launch vehicle into space.

radar Radio detection and ranging. A system for calculating the distance and direction of objects such as ships, planes and stormclouds. A transmitter sends out bursts of radio waves which bounce off objects, and the reflected 'radio echoes' can then be analysed.

radiation Energy emitted either in the form of rays of the electromagnetic spectrum, or particles such as electrons and neutrons.

radio waves Waves of the electromagnetic spectrum. They have wavelengths of up to one kilometre or more and are used in many forms of communication, such as broadcast radio, television, radar and navigation.

scramble To send signals or information using a secret code, so that others cannot know what is being sent.

sextant A navigational device that measures the positions and angles of the Sun, Moon, stars and other objects.

transponder A device carried by satellites that receives, strengthens and sends on radio signals. It may also be used to check that a satellite is in the correct orbit and working normally.

ultraviolet Waves of the electromagnetic spectrum that are shorter than the shortest or violet waves of visible light. We cannot see them, though some animals, such as bees, can.

X-rays Waves of the electromagnetic spectrum used in medicine to 'see into' the body. Many stars and other objects in space give off very weak X-rays.

FIND OUT MORE

Books to read

Book of the Universe by Ian Ridpath (Dragon's World, 1991)
The Space Atlas by Heather Couper and Nigel Henbest (Dorling Kindersley, 1992)
Space Travel by Robin Kerrod (Wayland, 1991)
Super Science Book of Space by Jerry Wellington (Wayland, 1993)
Telesatellite by Mat Irvine (Franklin Watts, 1989)

Places to visit

Cape Canaveral and Kennedy Space Center, Florida, USA
The world's most famous space launching site, with public displays and tours about all aspects of rocketry, spacecraft and satellites.

National Air and Space Museum (part of Smithsonian Institution), Washington DC, USA
Exhibits covering the whole subject of sky and space, from the Wright brothers' first airplane to the Apollo moonships, plus many satellites.

The Science Museum, Exhibition Road, London, UK
Many exhibits about rockets, satellites and other spacecraft.

The Planetarium, Euston Road, London, UK
Programmes about space, planets, stars and how they are explored by spacecraft, probes and satellites.

INDEX

48